Threads of Tsugai Embroidery

A Practical Guide to Japanese Counted Embroidery

Kenny K. Johnson

Table Of Content:

Introduction

Welcome to *Threads of Tsugaru: Kogin Embroidery*. This book is your guide to one of Japan's most distinctive textile arts Kogin, a counted-thread embroidery tradition that originated in the snowy Tsugaru region of northern Japan. Originally developed as a practical method to reinforce and warm clothing, Kogin has evolved into a beautiful art form, celebrated for its geometric patterns, careful precision, and timeless elegance.

Whether you are a beginner eager to learn the basics or an experienced stitcher looking to explore traditional Japanese motifs, this book combines history, technique, and hands-on projects to help you master Kogin. You will discover how to read patterns, select materials, and create your own designs, while connecting with the rich cultural heritage behind every stitch.

By the end of this guide, you won't just know how to stitch you'll understand the stories, the rhythm, and the spirit that make Kogin embroidery a living art form.

Chapter One:

The History and Spirit of Kogin

Origins in the Tsugaru Region

Kogin embroidery, also known as *Kogin-zashi*, originated in the Tsugaru region of northern Japan, in what is now Aomori Prefecture. This area is known for its harsh winters, with heavy snowfall and freezing temperatures. Historically, the local population relied on practical measures to survive the cold, including layering garments made from cotton or hemp. Because cotton was expensive and difficult to obtain, the Tsugaru people developed a method to reinforce their clothing with counted-thread stitching.

Kogin stitching involved applying layers of running stitches over worn or fragile fabric, particularly the indigo-dyed hemp or cotton jackets worn by farmers and fishermen. This technique not only strengthened the cloth but also added insulation, making it functional as well as visually appealing. The repetition of geometric patterns ensured even reinforcement, creating durable garments that could withstand daily wear in challenging conditions.

Connection to Japanese Culture and Aesthetics

Beyond its practical function, Kogin embroidery reflects a distinctly Japanese aesthetic. The art values simplicity, symmetry, and subtle beauty principles deeply rooted in Japanese culture. The geometric motifs, often squares, diamonds, or crosses, echo the Japanese appreciation for order, balance, and harmony with nature.

Kogin is also linked to the Japanese concept of *wabi-sabi*, the appreciation of imperfection and impermanence. Although the stitching patterns are precise, minor variations in thread tension or alignment are seen as part of the charm, giving each piece a unique character. By blending utility with beauty, Kogin represents a culture in which artistry emerges naturally from everyday life, rather than existing separately in galleries or exhibitions.

Evolution from Practical Stitching to Decorative Art

Over time, Kogin embroidery evolved from a purely functional practice into a decorative and expressive art form. As the cost of cotton decreased and clothing became more accessible, the reinforcement function became less critical. Artisans began to focus more on pattern variety and aesthetic appeal.

Modern Kogin retains its traditional geometric motifs but incorporates new color palettes, fabric choices, and creative interpretations. Contemporary stitchers use Kogin for home décor, fashion accents, and art pieces, expanding its presence far beyond northern Japan. This evolution demonstrates the adaptability of traditional crafts, proving that practical techniques can transform into enduring artistic expressions.

Symbolism of Patterns and Motifs

Each Kogin pattern carries symbolic meaning, often reflecting aspects of nature, community, and life in northern Japan. Common motifs include:

- **Diamonds and squares:** Represent stability, protection, and strength, echoing the reinforcing function of the stitches.

- **Crosses and grids:** Symbolize harmony and order, reinforcing the Japanese value of balance in everyday life.

- **Vertical and horizontal lines:** Evoke elements of the natural landscape, such as rice fields or snowy landscapes.

While these designs originated for functional reasons, they also became a language of identity and pride. Families and villages developed signature motifs, allowing wearers to signal origin or skill level through their stitching.

Famous Historical Examples

Historical examples of Kogin embroidery are preserved in museums and private collections in Japan. One notable example is the traditional indigo jacket, or *hanten*, worn by Tsugaru farmers in the 18th and 19th centuries. These garments display meticulous geometric stitching covering elbows, shoulders, and cuffs, demonstrating both functional reinforcement and aesthetic consideration.

Another example includes ceremonial garments used in local festivals, which combine Kogin stitching with vibrant threads and elaborate motifs. Such pieces highlight the evolution of Kogin from a survival tool to a cultural art form.

These historical artifacts provide modern stitchers with inspiration and a connection to the heritage of Tsugaru, emphasizing that every stitch carries centuries of tradition and human ingenuity.

Chapter Two:

Understanding Kogin Basics

What Is Counted-Thread Embroidery?

Counted-thread embroidery is a technique in which stitches are made by counting the threads of the fabric rather than following a pre-drawn design. Each stitch covers a specific number of warp and weft threads, allowing for precise geometric patterns and symmetry.

Kogin embroidery belongs to this category. It relies on careful counting to create repetitive patterns, often forming diamonds, squares, and crosses. Unlike freehand embroidery, counted-thread techniques require attention to detail, but they also offer consistency and structure. This approach is ideal for reinforcing fabric because the stitches are evenly spaced, creating both strength and beauty in the textile.

Difference Between Kogin and Other Japanese Embroidery Forms

Japan has several traditional embroidery styles, each with distinct techniques and purposes. Two of the most commonly compared forms are Kogin and Sashiko:

- **Kogin Embroidery**

  o Origin: Tsugaru region, northern Japan

  o Purpose: Originally reinforcement of clothing; later evolved into decorative art

  o Design: Geometric patterns, primarily horizontal or diagonal stitches on indigo-dyed fabric

  o Technique: Uses a running stitch, counted precisely across the threads of the fabric

- **Sashiko Embroidery**

  o Origin: Broader regions of Japan, including farming communities

  o Purpose: Strengthen and repair garments also decorative

- Design: Often linear, repetitive motifs, more open and spaced than Kogin

- Technique: Running stitch, often with larger spacing and simpler geometric motifs

While both styles share historical roots in functional stitching, Kogin is characterized by denser, more intricate patterns, often covering large areas of the fabric, whereas Sashiko tends to emphasize simplicity and elegance.

Materials Needed

To start Kogin embroidery, you need a few essential materials. Selecting the right supplies will affect both the ease of stitching and the final appearance of your projects:

1. **Fabric**

- Traditional: Indigo-dyed cotton or hemp, loosely woven to allow clear thread counting

- Modern alternatives: Linen or even weave cotton suitable for counted-thread work

- Consider color contrast: light thread on dark fabric is most traditional

2. Threads

- Cotton threads are most common; traditionally white or off-white

- Modern options: colored threads for contemporary designs

- Thickness: Two-ply or six-ply embroidery floss depending on desired texture

3. Needles

- Embroidery or tapestry needles with a blunt tip are ideal

- The needle should be long enough to pass through fabric easily but fine enough to avoid splitting threads

4. **Hoops or Frames**

- Maintain even tension while stitching

- Small hoops for detailed work, larger frames for bigger pieces

5. **Other Tools**

- Scissors: sharp and small for precise thread trimming

- Measuring tape or ruler: helpful when planning patterns

- Pins or clips to hold fabric in place

How to Read Kogin Patterns

Kogin patterns are **grid-based**, meaning each square on a chart represents a stitch on the fabric. Understanding these patterns is essential before starting your first project:

- **Grids**:

  o Horizontal and vertical lines on the pattern correspond to the threads in the fabric

  o Each square equals a single stitch, helping maintain symmetry

- **Motifs**:

  o Traditional motifs are repeated sequences of squares forming geometric shapes

  o Examples include diamonds, crosses, and zigzags

- Some motifs carry symbolic meaning, such as protection, prosperity, or harmony

- **Counting Stitches**:

  - Count fabric threads carefully before stitching

  - Begin at the center of the fabric or pattern for balanced designs

  - Keep consistent tension to maintain uniform stitch size

Key Terminology

Familiarity with common Kogin terms helps make instructions and patterns easier to follow:

- **Warp and Weft**: The vertical (warp) and horizontal (weft) threads of the fabric

- **Running Stitch**: The basic stitch used in Kogin, moving in a straight line over counted threads

- **Motif**: A repeated design or symbol within a pattern

- **Grid**: The chart that represents the fabric threads for counted stitching

- **Tsugaru**: The northern region of Japan where Kogin originated

- **Hanten**: Traditional indigo-dyed jackets often embroidered with Kogin.

Chapter Three:

Preparing Your Materials

Choosing the Right Fabric

Selecting the right fabric is one of the most important steps in Kogin embroidery. The fabric must allow counted-thread stitching while providing durability and a smooth surface for even stitches.

- **Linen:**

  Linen is a natural, breathable fabric

with a clear weave, making it easy to count threads. It is strong and ages beautifully, giving finished pieces a traditional look. Its slightly textured surface also adds depth to the stitches.

- **Cotton:**
Cotton is widely used due to its accessibility and ease of handling. Even weave cotton works particularly well for Kogin, as it has evenly spaced threads both vertically and horizontally. Cotton comes in a variety of weights and finishes, allowing versatility for different projects.

- **Indigo-Dyed Cloth:**
Indigo-dyed fabrics are historically authentic to Kogin, reflecting the tradition of Tsugaru. The deep blue

background enhances the contrast with white or light-colored threads, making geometric patterns stand out beautifully. Modern indigo fabrics vary in saturation and softness, giving stitchers options for contemporary designs.

Tips:

- Choose a tightly woven fabric that is still easy to count threads through.

- Pre-wash fabrics to prevent shrinkage after stitching.

- Consider fabric color contrast: traditional Kogin uses light thread on dark cloth, but modern variations are also visually striking.

Selecting Threads

The choice of thread affects both the look and feel of your Kogin embroidery.

- **Colors:**

    Traditional Kogin uses white or off-white cotton thread against indigo-dyed fabric. Contemporary designs may incorporate shades of blue, red, or even metallic threads for creative flair. Choosing high-contrast threads ensures your geometric patterns remain clear and precise.

- **Thickness:**

    Thread thickness influences the texture and coverage of your stitches. A two-ply thread offers delicate, subtle detail, while a six-ply embroidery floss produces bolder, more pronounced stitches. It is important to maintain consistency in thickness throughout a project to preserve pattern uniformity.

- **Traditional vs. Modern Threads:** Traditional threads are typically cotton or silk and reflect the historical aesthetic. Modern threads may include synthetic blends that are more durable or come in expanded color ranges. While modern threads offer creative flexibility, they may behave differently under tension, so testing on a sample piece is recommended.

Needles and Tools

Using the right tools is essential for smooth, accurate stitching.

- **Needles:**

  o Embroidery needles with blunt tips are preferred for Kogin because they pass between threads without splitting them.

○ A medium-length needle is versatile for both small and large projects.

○ Keep a variety of sizes available for different thread thicknesses and fabric densities.

- **Hoops and Frames:**

○ Hoops help maintain consistent tension, preventing puckering or uneven stitches.

○ Small hoops are ideal for detailed work, while larger frames are suited for bigger textiles.

○ Wooden or plastic hoops work well; choose what feels comfortable in your hands.

- **Additional Tools:**

- Sharp scissors for precise thread cutting

- Measuring tape or ruler for planning patterns

- Pins or clips to secure fabric edges

- Light pencil or erasable fabric marker (optional) for marking pattern guides

Preparing Your Workspace

A well-prepared workspace improves stitching efficiency and comfort.

- **Lighting:**

- Good lighting is essential, especially when working with dark fabrics or fine threads.

- Natural daylight is ideal; otherwise, use bright, adjustable desk lamps.

- **Frame and Positioning:**

  o Secure your fabric in a hoop or frame to maintain even tension.

  o Keep the work at eye level or slightly below to reduce neck strain.

- **Ergonomics:**

  o Sit in a comfortable chair with back support.

  o Take breaks to stretch fingers, hands, and shoulders.

  o Organize your threads and tools within easy reach to avoid repetitive movements.

Understanding Tension and Stitch Consistency

Tension is the foundation of neat, even Kogin stitches. Uneven tension can distort patterns, cause puckering, or create inconsistent texture.

- **Maintaining Even Tension:**

  o Pull each stitch gently and consistently.

  o Avoid tugging too tightly, which can warp the fabric, or leaving stitches too loose, which can look messy.

- **Consistency Tips:**

  o Practice on a small swatch before starting a full project.

  o Check frequently that stitches align with the fabric threads and the pattern grid.

  o Keep the fabric taut in your hoop or frame throughout the stitching process.

Chapter Four:

Essential Kogin Stitches

Kogin embroidery relies on a few fundamental stitches repeated in geometric patterns. Once you master these, you can create intricate designs and add texture to your projects. This chapter guides you step by step, with clear instructions suitable for beginners.

The Basic Running Stitch

The running stitch is the backbone of Kogin embroidery. It is a straight stitch that passes over a counted number of threads on the fabric.

Step-by-Step Instructions:

1. Thread your needle and knot the end.

2. Bring the needle up through the fabric at your starting point.

3. Count a set number of threads along the fabric (usually 2–4) and insert the needle back down.

4. Repeat this process, keeping the length of each stitch uniform.

Tips:

- Keep stitches even in length for consistent patterns.

- Maintain gentle tension; avoid pulling too tight or leaving threads loose.

Running Stitch Variations

Kogin embroidery uses variations of the basic running stitch to create pattern diversity.

1. **Double Running Stitch**

   - Stitch forward along your counted threads, then return along the same path to fill gaps.

   - Produces a continuous, solid line that looks uniform from both sides.

2. **Interrupted Running Stitch**

   - Leave small gaps between groups of stitches.

   - Useful for creating textured motifs or borders.

3. **Stacked Running Stitch**

- ○ Two or more stitches are placed directly on top of each other for added thickness.

- ○ Ideal for emphasis in patterns like diamonds or crosses.

Horizontal, Vertical, and Diagonal Patterns

Kogin designs rely on arranging stitches in **different directions** to form geometric patterns:

- **Horizontal Lines:**

- ○ Stitch across the width of the fabric, keeping thread count consistent.

- ○ Creates stripes or grids in your pattern.

- **Vertical Lines:**

- Stitch along the fabric's vertical threads.

- Can intersect horizontal stitches to form squares or rectangles.

- **Diagonal Lines:**

- Stitch at a 45-degree angle across counted threads.

- Used for diamonds, zigzags, and more intricate motifs.

Combining Stitches for Texture and Dimension

Combining stitches in different directions and densities creates **visual depth** in Kogin embroidery:

- **Grid Fill:** Alternate horizontal and vertical stitches in squares to fill a block.

- **Diamond Motif:** Use diagonal stitches in alternating directions to form repeating diamonds.

- **Layered Effects:** Stack running stitches over a previous layer for emphasis, creating raised patterns.

Tip: Always plan the sequence of stitches on paper or a small sample before applying them to your main project.

Troubleshooting Common Stitch Errors

Even beginners encounter mistakes. Here's how to fix them:

1. **Uneven Stitch Lengths:**

   o Solution: Count threads carefully, and use a hoop to maintain tension.

2. **Twisted Threads:**

- o Solution: Allow thread to hang freely every few stitches to untwist, or roll it gently between fingers.

3. **Fabric Puckering:**

- o Solution: Avoid pulling stitches too tight; keep the fabric taut but relaxed in a hoop.

4. **Misaligned Patterns:**

- o Solution: Mark grid lines lightly with a pencil or fabric marker before stitching.

- o Correct errors by carefully unpicking and restitching.

Practice Exercises for Confidence

Before starting a full project, practice these exercises:

1. **Simple Horizontal Stripe:**

- Count 3 threads per stitch and make a horizontal line across 20 stitches.

2. **Vertical Grid:**

- On a small square, stitch vertical lines intersecting your horizontal stripe to form a grid.

3. **Diamond Shape:**

- Use diagonal stitches to form a simple diamond motif. Repeat 3–4 times across a sample square.

4. **Stacked Line:**

- Layer two rows of horizontal stitches directly on top of each other to feel the raised effect.

5. **Combined Motif:**

- Create a small sample combining horizontal, vertical, and diagonal stitches to see how patterns interlock.

Tip: Practice on a scrap piece of fabric. Mistakes here are part of learning and will give confidence for real projects.

Chapter Five:

Reading and Creating Patterns

Kogin embroidery is distinguished by its geometric, counted-thread designs. Learning to read charts and create your own motifs is essential for both replicating traditional patterns and exploring modern creativity. This chapter guides you through reading traditional charts, translating them to fabric, and designing original motifs inspired by Tsugaru's heritage.

How to Read Traditional Kogin Charts

Traditional Kogin patterns are typically presented as **grid-based charts**. Each square on the chart corresponds to a stitch on the fabric. Understanding these charts ensures your stitches are precise and your patterns symmetrical.

- **Grid Layout:**

  o Vertical lines on the chart represent the warp threads of the fabric.

  o Horizontal lines represent the weft threads.

  o Each filled square indicates where to place a stitch. Empty squares represent spaces without stitching.

42

- **Symbols and Shading:**

  ○ Some charts use symbols, shading, or colors to indicate stitch direction or thread color.

  ○ Dark squares may indicate horizontal stitches; light squares may indicate vertical or diagonal stitches.

- **Pattern Repetition:**

  ○ Many Kogin patterns are designed as repeats. Look for the smallest unit of the pattern that repeats horizontally or vertically.

  ○ Repeating motifs maintain balance and harmony across a larger fabric area.

Tip: Start with simple charts before moving to complex patterns. Practice reading charts while counting threads on a small fabric swatch.

Translating Patterns to Fabric

Once you understand a chart, transferring it to fabric involves careful counting and planning:

1. **Choose Starting Point:**

   - Begin at the center of your fabric or the pattern for balanced results.

   - For smaller motifs, starting from a corner may also work.

2. **Counting Threads:**

   - Count the warp and weft threads carefully to match the chart's grid.

   - Keep stitches consistent in length and direction.

3. **Marking Guidelines (Optional):**

- Use a light pencil, fabric marker, or basting thread to outline the main grid or motif areas.

- Helps prevent misalignment, especially for larger patterns.

4. **Follow the Chart Step by Step:**

- Work one row or column at a time.

- Cross-check each stitch with the chart before continuing.

5. **Check Alignment:**

- Pause periodically to ensure the stitches match the intended motif and symmetry.

Designing Your Own Motifs Inspired by Tsugaru

Kogin tradition allows for creative interpretation. Designing original motifs involves blending heritage with personal expression:

1. **Start with Inspiration:**

   - Observe traditional Tsugaru motifs: diamonds, crosses, zigzags, and grid fills.

   - Consider natural or cultural elements from the region: snow, rice fields, waves, or family symbols.

2. **Sketch on Graph Paper:**

   - Draw motifs using a square grid to simulate fabric threads.

   - Each square represents a stitch, making it easy to test symmetry and repetition.

3. **Combine Simple Shapes:**

- Experiment with layering diamonds over horizontal stripes or alternating zigzags and crosses.

- Repetition is key: repeated units create rhythm and balance in Kogin embroidery.

4. **Test Small Swatches:**

- Transfer the motif to a scrap fabric before committing to a full project.

- Adjust spacing, stitch length, or direction as needed.

Grid Mapping for Beginners

Beginners can use grid mapping to simplify pattern translation:

- **Step 1:** Draw a basic grid on graph paper matching your fabric's thread count.

- **Step 2:** Shade or mark squares to represent where stitches will go.

- **Step 3:** Transfer small sections at a time to the fabric, counting threads carefully.

- **Step 4:** Keep a ruler or straight edge handy for alignment, especially on larger pieces.

This method reduces mistakes, makes patterns easier to follow, and builds confidence for more complex designs.

Tips for Combining Traditional and Modern Aesthetics

Modern Kogin embroidery often merges classic motifs with contemporary ideas:

- **Color Variations:** Use unexpected thread colors while keeping traditional patterns intact.

- **Fabric Choices:** Experiment with modern fabrics (linen blends, even weave cotton in neutral or pastel tones) for a fresh look.

- **Pattern Fusion:** Mix small traditional motifs into larger, abstract compositions.

- **Layering and Texture:** Combine stacked stitches, overlapping shapes, or varying stitch densities to add depth.

Tip: Respect the symmetry and balance of traditional Kogin while exploring creative deviations. Small experiments often yield striking results.

Practice Exercises

1. **Simple Diamond Repeat:** Sketch a diamond motif on graph paper, then

stitch a row of 5–6 repeats on a small swatch.

2. **Mixed Motif Strip:** Combine horizontal and diagonal lines in a short strip to understand interaction of different stitch directions.

3. **Color Play:** Take a classic white-on-indigo motif and try stitching it with two contrasting colors to see the effect.

4. **Personal Symbol:** Create a small 3×3 motif inspired by nature or culture, test it on scrap fabric, and evaluate symmetry.

Chapter Six:

Small Projects to Start With

Once you've learned the basic stitches and how to read patterns, the next step is to practice on **small, manageable projects**. These allow you to gain confidence, understand stitch spacing, and experience the satisfaction of completing a finished piece without feeling overwhelmed.

This chapter covers **coasters, bookmarks, and small decorative**

panels, providing step-by-step guidance and beginner-friendly patterns.

1. Simple Kogin Coasters

Materials Needed:

- 4×4 inch scrap of indigo-dyed cotton or linen
- White cotton embroidery thread
- Embroidery needle and hoop
- Scissors

Step-by-Step Instructions:

1. Secure the fabric in a hoop.

2. Draw a 4×4 grid lightly on the fabric (optional) for guidance.

3. Select a simple motif, like a diamond or square.

Example:

Start from the center of the coaster and work outward, following the grid.

4. Complete one motif per coaster or repeat the motif to fill the square.

5. Finish the edges by folding ¼ inch fabric inward and stitching down with small running stitches or overcast stitch.

Tips:

- Keep stitches uniform in length for a neat appearance.

- Coasters are ideal for practicing tension and consistency.

2. Kogin Bookmark

Materials Needed:

- 2×6 inch strip of fabric

- White or light-colored embroidery thread

- Needle, hoop (optional)

- Ribbon or fabric strip for finishing ends

Step-by-Step Instructions:

1. Place the fabric in a hoop for stability.

2. Choose a linear motif, such as horizontal stripes or repeating diamonds.

Example:

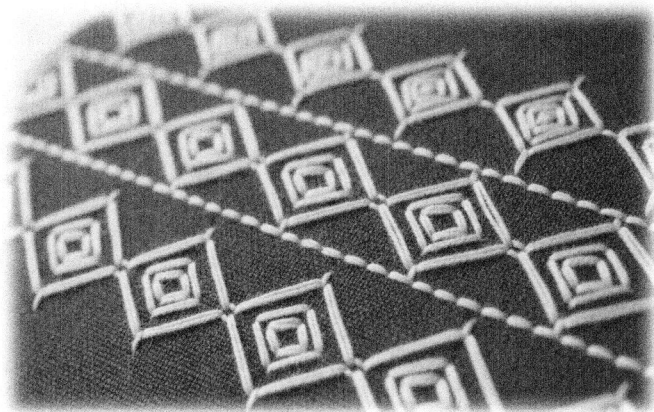

Count fabric threads carefully and stitch row by row.

3. Continue until the bookmark reaches desired length.

4. Finish ends by folding ¼ inch inward and stitching, or attach a ribbon to one end for decoration.

Tips:

• Use contrasting thread to make patterns stand out.

- Linear projects help you practice even stitch spacing and pattern repetition.

3. Small Decorative Panels

Materials Needed:

- 6×6 inch square of linen or cotton

- Embroidery threads (1–2 colors)

- Needle, hoop

- Optional backing fabric for finishing

Step-by-Step Instructions:

1. Secure fabric in a hoop.

2. Select a motif that fills the square, such as a central diamond surrounded by diagonal lines.

Example:

3. Begin stitching from the center motif, moving outward symmetrically.

4. Once the motif is complete, add small border stitches around the edges if desired.

5. Optional: Attach a backing fabric by stitching along the edges to hide raw threads.

Tips:

- Decorative panels are perfect for experimenting with combining horizontal, vertical, and diagonal stitches.

- Using a hoop ensures stitches remain even across the panel.

Choosing Beginner-Friendly Patterns

- Start with **simple geometric motifs**: squares, diamonds, crosses.

- Limit the number of colors to one or two for clarity.

- Avoid overly intricate designs until you feel confident with counting and stitch consistency.

- Repeat small motifs rather than trying large, complex ones immediately.

Tips for Finishing Edges and Backing

1. **Edges:**

- Fold the fabric edge ¼ inch inward and secure with small running or overcast stitches.

- This prevents fraying and gives a clean, polished look.

2. **Backing:**

- For coasters and panels, you can attach a plain cotton or felt backing for extra stability.

- Stitch along the edge to secure and hide raw threads.

- Press lightly with an iron to flatten the finished piece.

3. **General Care:**

o   Trim excess threads carefully.

o   Wash completed projects gently by hand to preserve color and thread texture.

Practice Exercises

1. Make **a set of four coasters** using the same simple motif, focusing on consistent tension.

2. Create **two bookmarks** with different linear patterns to practice horizontal and diagonal stitches.

3. Design **a small panel** combining two motifs you learned, experimenting with spacing and symmetry.

Chapter Seven:

Intermediate Projects

After mastering basic stitches and small projects, you can move on to **intermediate Kogin embroidery projects**. These involve larger surfaces, multiple motifs, and sometimes color variations. Table runners, cushion covers, and small clothing accents provide opportunities to practice design planning, stitch consistency, and combining motifs.

1. Table Runner

Materials Needed:

- Fabric: 12×36 inches of linen, cotton, or indigo-dyed cloth

- Threads: 1–2 colors, cotton embroidery floss

- Embroidery needle, hoop or frame

- Scissors, measuring tape, pins

Step-by-Step Instructions:

1. **Plan Your Design:**

   o Sketch the runner layout on graph paper or draw lightly on fabric.

   o Choose 2–3 motifs to repeat along the length, such as alternating diamonds and crosses.

2. **Centering the Motifs:**

- Find the center of the fabric lengthwise.

- Begin stitching from the center outward to maintain symmetry.

3. **Stitch the Main Motifs:**

- Use counted-thread technique for each motif.

- Example of a diamond motif in text diagram form:

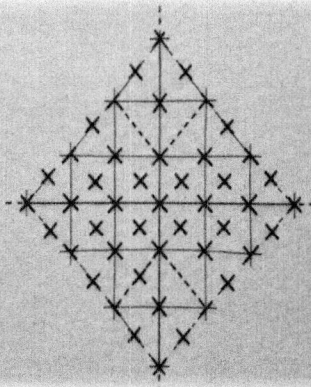

4. **Add Borders:**

- Surround motifs with horizontal or vertical line borders.

- Borders unify the design and keep pattern repetition aligned.

5. **Finishing:**

- Fold edges ¼ inch inward and stitch or hem.

- Optional: attach a backing for extra stability.

Tips:

- Break the project into sections to avoid fatigue.

- Count threads frequently to maintain alignment across the runner.

2. Cushion Cover

Materials Needed:

- Fabric: 14×14 inch square for front, 14×14 inch square for back

- Thread: 1–2 colors

- Needle, hoop, scissors

- Sewing machine or hand-sewing tools for assembly

Step-by-Step Instructions:

1. **Choose Motifs:**

o Select a central motif and 1–2 smaller surrounding motifs.

o Example: central diamond with corner cross motifs.

2. **Position the Motifs:**

o Lightly mark the fabric with pencil to guide placement.

3. **Stitch the Motifs:**

o   Begin with the central motif, then stitch surrounding motifs.

o   Maintain even tension and spacing.

4. **Add Borders (Optional):**

o   Horizontal or vertical lines along edges enhance the overall pattern.

5. **Assemble the Cushion:**

o   Place front and back pieces together, right sides facing out.

o   Stitch edges, leaving one side open to insert a cushion.

o   Turn inside out, insert cushion, and stitch the remaining edge closed.

Tips:

- Use contrasting thread to make motifs pop against the fabric.

- For multi-colored designs, plan thread transitions to minimize knotting.

3. Small Clothing Accents

Ideas:

- Pockets, cuffs, collars, or small patches.

Materials Needed:

- Fabric scraps from garment or coordinating material
- Threads, needle, hoop (optional)
- Pins, scissors

Step-by-Step Instructions:

1. **Select a Motif:**

   o Choose a small motif that fits the accent area.

- Example: a 3×3 diamond motif or a small grid pattern.

2. **Position and Pin:**

- Place the motif on the desired area (pocket, cuff, etc.)
- Pin securely to prevent movement during stitching.

3. **Stitch the Motif:**

- Use counted-thread technique; work slowly to maintain symmetry.
- Ensure motifs are centered and aligned.

4. **Finish Edges:**

- For patches, fold edges under and stitch down or attach using appliqué technique.

o For collars or cuffs, ensure stitches are neat and secure.

Tips:

- Pre-wash garment fabric to avoid shrinking after stitching.

- Small accents allow experimentation with color variations and layering stitches.

Combining Multiple Motifs in One Design

Intermediate projects often require combining motifs to create visual interest:

1. **Plan the Layout:**

o Sketch motifs on paper or lightly on fabric.

o Consider symmetry, spacing, and balance.

2. **Sequence of Stitching:**

○ Start with the central or largest motif.

○ Add secondary motifs around it to maintain harmony.

3. **Maintain Tension and Alignment:**

○ Count threads carefully between motifs.

○ Check periodically that motifs remain aligned.

Incorporating Color Variations and Shading

1. **Color Choices:**

○ Traditional Kogin uses light thread on dark fabric, but you can add one or two additional colors for depth.

2. **Shading Techniques:**

o Use slightly lighter or darker shades of a color to create subtle depth in motifs.

o Work diagonal stitches with alternating shades to create a gradient effect.

3. **Planning Transitions:**

o Test color combinations on a small swatch before applying to the main project.

Project Timelines and Tips for Efficiency

- **Break Work Into Sections:** Work on one motif or section at a time.

- **Set Goals:** Commit to completing a small portion each day.

- **Keep Materials Organized:** Thread, needles, and scissors within easy reach.

- **Use a Hoop or Frame:** Helps maintain tension and reduces fatigue.

- **Take Breaks:** Stretch hands, shoulders, and neck every 30–45 minutes.

Chapter Eight:

Kogin Creations

As your skills in Kogin embroidery grow, you can begin tackling **larger, more ambitious projects**. This chapter explores creating wall hangings, bags, and garments, using complex traditional Tsugaru patterns while experimenting with modern techniques. You'll also learn how historical examples can inspire contemporary designs.

1. Larger Textiles: Wall Hangings, Bags, and Garments

Wall Hangings:

- **Materials:** Linen or cotton fabric (18×24 inches or larger), embroidery threads, hoop or frame, dowel for hanging.

- **Design Planning:** Sketch motifs on graph paper first. Traditional repeats, large diamonds, or multiple motif combinations work well for vertical or horizontal layouts.

- **Step-by-Step:**

1. Secure fabric in a frame for stability.

2. Begin stitching from the center of your main motif.

3. Add surrounding patterns, keeping spacing and alignment consistent.

4. Finish edges by hemming or adding backing fabric for a polished appearance.

5. Attach a dowel or rod to the top for hanging.

Bags:

- **Materials:** Medium-weight fabric, threads, lining fabric, zipper or drawstring, needle, hoop.

- **Design Planning:** Choose a motif suitable for the bag's size. Central motifs or repeated small patterns work well.

- **Step-by-Step:**

1. Stitch the exterior panel first, completing all motifs before assembly.

2. Cut lining fabric to match the stitched piece.

3. Assemble bag pieces, ensuring motifs are centered and straight.

4. Sew edges and attach closures.

Garments:

- Small accents like collars, cuffs, pockets, or panels are ideal for beginner garment projects.

- Larger garments, such as vests or jackets, allow for extensive motif combinations and layering.

- **Step-by-Step:**

1. Identify areas for Kogin embroidery.

2. Mark fabric lightly for motif placement.

3. Stitch motifs carefully, checking symmetry and tension.

4. Finish with neat seams and optional backing for durability.

2. Complex Patterns: Traditional Tsugaru Designs

Tsugaru Kogin motifs are intricate, often combining geometric shapes, diagonal lines, and stacked stitches. To work with complex patterns:

1. **Study Historical Patterns:**

   o Observe museum examples or high-quality photos of Tsugaru garments.

   o Note how diamonds, crosses, and zigzags are layered.

2. **Break Down the Pattern:**

   o Divide large patterns into smaller repeatable units.

- Work section by section to maintain accuracy.

3. **Count Carefully:**

- Miscounted stitches can distort symmetry in complex designs.

- Use markers or light pencil lines for guidance.

4. **Combine Motifs:**

- Alternate motif sizes to create rhythm.

- Mix horizontal, vertical, and diagonal lines for depth and texture.

Example of a Layered Diamond Motif:

3. Mixing Traditional Stitches with Modern Techniques

Advanced Kogin embroidery can combine historical methods with contemporary embroidery techniques:

- **Layering:** Use stacked or overlapping stitches to create raised patterns.

- **Mixed Stitching:** Combine running stitches with satin, backstitch, or French knots for texture.

- **Thread Variations:** Introduce metallic or variegated threads while maintaining traditional pattern structure.

- **Negative Space:** Leave intentional unstitched areas to modernize a classic motif.

Tip: Always experiment on a small swatch before applying new techniques to a full piece.

4. Inspiration from Historical Kogin Examples

Historical Kogin garments, particularly those from the Tsugaru region, provide invaluable inspiration:

- **Repeating Diamonds:** Common in traditional jackets, symbolizing protection and continuity.

- **Stacked Lines:** Originally used for fabric reinforcement, now a textural design element.

- **Motif Symbolism:** Crosses and zigzags may represent family, community, or natural elements.

How to Adapt:

- Scale motifs up or down for modern projects.

- Integrate classic patterns into contemporary items like tote bags, pillow covers, or wall hangings.

- Maintain the aesthetic balance of symmetry and repetition characteristic of Tsugaru Kogin.

Project Planning Tips for Large Pieces

- **Start Small:** Even in a large project, begin with a central motif before expanding.

- **Work in Sections:** Divide the fabric into grids for easier pattern management.

- **Keep Organized:** Label threads and motifs to prevent confusion in multi-color projects.

- **Set Milestones:** Completing sections daily or weekly keeps motivation high.

- **Test Swatches:** Always try new combinations of stitches, colors, or layers on a small piece first.

Chapter Nine:

Caring for Your Kogin Creations

Creating beautiful Kogin embroidery is only part of the journey. Proper care ensures your pieces **retain their beauty, shape, and color** for years to come. This chapter covers washing, storage, repairs, and display ideas.

1. Washing and Preserving Embroidered Textiles

- **Hand Washing:**

  o Fill a basin with lukewarm water and a mild detergent or soap specifically for delicate fabrics.

  o Gently submerge your Kogin piece and lightly agitate the water. Avoid rubbing the fabric or scrubbing stitches.

  o Rinse thoroughly with cool water to remove all soap.

- **Drying:**

  o Lay the piece flat on a clean towel, gently pressing out excess water.

  o Avoid wringing, twisting, or hanging while wet, as this can distort the fabric and stitches.

- Air dry away from direct sunlight to prevent fading, especially on indigo-dyed fabrics.

- **Ironing:**

- Iron on the reverse side, using a low to medium heat setting.

- Place a thin cloth or pressing sheet between the iron and the embroidery to protect threads.

2. Storing Projects to Maintain Shape and Color

- **Flat Storage:**

- Store small pieces like coasters, panels, or bookmarks flat in a drawer or storage box lined with acid-free tissue paper.

- Avoid folding heavily stitched areas to prevent creases.

- **Rolled Storage:**

  o For larger pieces like wall hangings or table runners, roll the fabric around a clean tube with tissue paper to prevent folds.

- **Avoid Humidity and Sunlight:**

  o Keep textiles in a cool, dry area to prevent mold, mildew, or fading.

  o Avoid prolonged exposure to sunlight, which can weaken fibers and alter colors.

3. Repairing or Modifying Older Pieces

- **Repairing Loose Threads:**

  o Gently tuck or stitch loose threads back into the pattern.

  o Use matching thread and maintain the original stitch direction.

- **Fixing Holes or Worn Areas:**

  ○ Patch from the reverse side using matching fabric and carefully stitch over damaged areas.

  ○ For minor wear, overlay a small decorative motif to disguise the area while maintaining style.

- **Modifying Designs:**

  ○ Add borders, extra motifs, or contrasting threads to refresh an older piece.

  ○ This can modernize a traditional textile while respecting the original design.

4. Display Ideas for Art and Functional Use

- **Wall Art:**

- Frame small panels or stretch larger textiles over canvas for a polished display.

- Rotate pieces seasonally to prevent long-term sunlight exposure.

- **Functional Use:**

- Coasters, cushion covers, table runners, and bags can showcase Kogin embroidery in everyday life.

- Use protective backing or linings to increase durability.

- **Combining Display and Preservation:**

- Use glass or acrylic frames for delicate pieces to protect from dust while highlighting patterns.

- Hang in areas away from heat sources, direct sunlight, and high humidity for longevity.

Conclusion

Kogin embroidery is more than a craft it is a living tradition that connects the hands of artisans today to the heritage of the Tsugaru region. Through mastering the basic stitches, learning to read and create patterns, and progressing to larger and more complex projects, you have explored both the technical and creative sides of this timeless art.

By practicing patience, precision, and creativity, you can transform simple threads and fabric into **beautiful, meaningful works**, whether for functional use or artistic display. Remember that each piece carries the spirit of Tsugaru, blending tradition with your personal expression.

As you continue your journey, let your stitches tell your story, honor the history behind the patterns, and inspire others to explore the **elegance and depth of Kogin embroidery**.

Printed in Dunstable, United Kingdom